# Practical Guide to the Operational Use of the Beretta 92/M9 Pistol

By Erik Lawrence

Copyright ©2014 Erik Lawrence

I0160059

Erik Lawrence
www.vig-sec.com    erik@vig-sec.com

**Printed and bound in the United States of America**

**First printing 2008**
**Second Printing 2014**

**ISBN-10: 1-941998-19-4**
**ISBN-13: 978-1-941998-19-9**
**EBOOK – ISBN-13: 978-1-941998-39-7**

**LCCN: Not yet assigned**

ATTENTION US MILITARY UNITS, US GOVERNMENT AGENCIES AND PROFESSIONAL ORGANIZATIONS: Quantity discounts are available on bulk purchases of this book. Special books or book excerpts can also be created to fit specific needs. For information, please contact:

Erik Lawrence
www.vig-sec.com    erik@vig-sec.com

SAFETY NOTICE
Before starting an inspection, ensure the weapon is cleared. Do not manipulate the trigger until the weapon has been cleared of all ammunition. Inspect the chamber to ensure that it is empty and no ammunition is present. Keep the weapon oriented in a safe direction when loading and handling.

AMMUNITION NOTICE- These weapons fire multiple types of grenades, and they must come from trusted sources; never fire captured grenades. Know the capabilities and limitation of each type of grenade. The 40mm grenades used in the MK19 grenade launcher (40 x 53mm) are not the same as in the M203 (40 x 46mm), which are fired at a lower velocity. Firing the incorrect ammunition will damage the weapon and possibly injure the operator/assistant operator.

Training should be received from knowledgeable and experienced operators on this particular weapons system. Vigilant Security Services, LCC Training provides this training and continually perfects its instruction with up-to-date information from actual use.

www.vig-sec.com

# Table of Contents

# Section 1

## Introduction

The objective of this manual is to allow the reader to be able to competently use the various Beretta pistols. The manual will give the reader background/specifications of the weapon, instructions on its operation, disassembly and assembly; proper firing procedure; and malfunction/misfire procedures. Operator level maintenance will also be detailed to allow the reader to understand and become competent in the use and maintenance of the Beretta 92F type pistol.

## Background

Originally designed for the Italian army and police, the Model 92 pistols earned most of their fame as the standard sidearm of the US military. It was developed between 1970 and 1975 as a possible replacement for ageing Beretta M951 pistol, and entered production in Italy in 1976. First adopted by the Brazilian army in 1977, this pistol was later adopted in Italy in its Model 92S, "SB", and finally "F" modifications. The US military adopted the Model 92SB-F (later renamed to model 92F) in 1985, as a result of the highly controversial XM9 trials. In the late 1980s and 1990s, these pistols were also adopted in France. It must be noted that, while being entirely adequate as a combat pistol, the Beretta 92 is somewhat bulky for its caliber and magazine capacity, thus less suitable for users with average or smaller hands. Other than the basic 9mm, Beretta also makes these pistols in other calibers, such as .40 S&W (model 96) and 9x21 IMI (Model 98, available for civilian users in certain European countries, including Italy). Beretta also makes a wide variety of models based on the same design; these include not only variations in finishes and sights, but also different trigger types (DA/SA, DA/SA with decock only, DAO, DAO with manual safety).

Designated the M9 Pistol in the U.S. Military system and interchangeable with 92FS

## Design

Beretta 92 pistols are short-recoil operated, locked-breech weapons with an aluminum frame. The locking system is of the Walther type, with a vertically-tilting locking piece located below the breech area of the barrel. The trigger is double-action, with an exposed hammer. Original Model 92 pistols had a frame-mounted safety which was applied only when hammer was cocked; all subsequent pistols (except for some limited production civilian-only sporting models) either had a slide-mounted safety lever or no safety lever at all. On some pistols, such as the Model 92G adopted in France, the levers do not lock themselves in the lowered position but return to the "FIRE" position once released – their function is limited

4

only to safe decocking of the hammer. Some other models, such as the Model 92D, are double-action-only pistols with no manual safety or decocker. All pistols of current production are fitted with an automatic firing pin block safety. Magazines are double stack, with the magazine release button located in the base of the trigger-guard on all 92-series pistols made since 1981. Sights on service models are of fixed type, with a dovetailed rear blade, usually with high-contrast inserts.

With the introduction of the Model 92FS in the late 1980s, another unusual safety feature was fitted in the form of an enlarged head to the hammer pin. The purpose of this safety is to prevent the rear of the slide from flying back into the firer's face in the case of the slide failure. This happened several times during the earlier years of Model 92F service in US military, apparently because of metallurgical problems, combined with the "built-in" weak points in the slide where the locking block cuts are made. Recognizing these weak points, the US INS (Immigration and Naturalization Service) requested Beretta to make their model 96 (.40 S&W caliber version of Model 92) with reinforced slides. This resulted in appearance of the Model 96 Brigadier pistols, and, later on, the same modification was applied to 9mm pistols, available as Model 92 Brigadier. Beretta also produced a number of compact versions of their basic, full-size Model 92 variations. These compact versions had shortened grips, slides and barrels; Compact Type M versions also featured single-stack magazines with appropriately thinned grips. At the present time, Beretta no longer makes Compact versions of the Model 92; in the firm's product line these were replaced by the entirely different Model 8000 Cougar pistols.

The newest military model is Model 92A1/M9A1 which has the Picatinny rail for using lights/lasers. More description is listed in the variants section later in the manual.

# Beretta 92FS/M9

**Figure 1-1 — Beretta 92FS/M9**

| | |
|---|---|
| **NSN** | **1005-01-118-2640** |
| **Caliber** | 9mm (9x19mm) |
| **Magazine Capacity** | 15 rounds – standard |
| **Overall Length** | 8.5"/ 217 mm |
| **Height** (Including Mag) | 5.4"/ 137 mm |
| **Width** | 1.5"/ 38 mm |
| **Sight Radius** | 6.1"/ 155 mm |
| **Barrel Length** | 4.9"/ 125 mm |
| **Barrel Rifling** | Right, Hexagonal |
| **Weight** (Without Mag) | 34.4 oz/ 975 g |
| **Action** | Double Action/Single Action |

# Beretta 92F Variants

**Beretta 92S** (1976) – first modification of the basic model 92, with non-ambidextrous slide-mounted safety/decocker and magazine release button set low in the left grip panel. It was replaced in production by the Model 92SB.

**Beretta 92SB** (1981) – further evolution of model 92S, initially designated Model 92S-1, later designated 92SB with the introduction of the firing pin block. The manual safety is ambidextrous, the magazine release relocated to the base of the trigger-guard. Discontinued since 1991.

**Beretta 92SB-C** (1981) – Compact version of the model 92SB. Overall length was 197 mm, barrel length 103 mm, magazine capacity 13 rounds (also accepted standard 15-round magazines).

**Beretta 92SB-C type M** (1983) – slimmer version of the model 92SB-C, with a single-stack magazine which held only 8 rounds.

**Beretta 92F** (1984) – initially designated 92SB-F, later renamed 92F. Evolved from the Model 92SB during American XM9 trials, with a slightly reshaped grip and trigger-guard, also a different finish. The barrel bore and chamber are chrome-plated.

**Beretta 92G** (1989)- the so called "Gendarmerie" version, created at the request of the Gendarmerie Nationale de France. These are also manufactured under license in France by GIAT Industries as the PA MAS G1. The pistol is the same as the model 92F except for the operations of the lever, which lost its safety lock function and is used only to safely decock the hammer.

**Beretta 92FS** (1989) – a minor modification of the Model 92F, with an enlarged hammer pin head which prevents the slide from flying back in the case of breakage. Presently, all US M9 pistols are modified to 92FS standard.

**Beretta 92FS-C** (1989) – compact version of the Model 92FS, similar in dimensions to earlier model 92SB-C. No longer made.

**Beretta 92FS-C type M** (1989) – single-stack version of Model 92FS-C, magazine capacity 8 rounds. No longer made.

**Beretta 92DS** (1990) – Double Action Only version of the Model 92FS, with spurless hammer and manual safety.

**Beretta 92D** (1990) Double Action Only version of the Model 92FS, with spurless hammer and no manual safety levers.

**Beretta 92FS Brigadier** (1996) – version of the Model 92FS with a reinforced, thickened slide; another change is that the front sight is not integral to the slide, but is dovetailed into it.

**Beretta 92FS Centurion** (1996) – version of the Model 92FS with a shortened barrel and slide, the frame is the same as on the Model 92FS. Overall length is 197 mm, barrel length is 103 mm, magazine capacity 15 rounds.

**Beretta 92 Vertec** (2003) – version of the Model 92FS that addressed constant complaints about the excessive grip width of Model 92 pistols. The backstrap of the grip on Vertec models is made more linear; another change is the addition of an integral Picatinny rail to the frame.

**Beretta 90two** (2006) - a most recent face-lift version of the basic Model 92 design. Key changes are modular one-piece grip panels (available in various shapes), integral Picatinny rail under the barrel (with cover), restyled slide and integral recoil buffer built into action.

**Beretta 92A1** (2010) - Combining the best elements of the 92FS and the 90-Two, these pistols feature higher capacity magazines: 17 rounds in 9x19mm. These are completely interchangeable with other 92 family magazines. It now has a removable front sight which allows the shooter to easily replace a damaged sight or replace it with an alternate sight. The frame of the new A1s has an integral MIL-STD-1913 Picatinny rail for rapid attachment of tactical lights and laser aiming devices. Captive recoil spring assembly in a single-piece design which simplifies the assembly and disassembly process and minimizes the possibility of spring loss. Rounded trigger guard and updated styling to conform to current pistol gripping practices.

**Figure 1-2 — Beretta 92A1/M9A1**

# Section 2

## Maintenance

## Clearing the Beretta Pistol

**Figure 2-1a — Safety – SAFE position**     **Figure 2-1b — Safety - FIRE position**

A. Ensure the pistol is pointed in a safe direction and finger off the trigger and out of the trigger guard.

**Figure 2-2a — Depress magazine release button**     **Figure 2-2b — Remove magazine**

B. Remove the magazine by pressing the magazine release button to the right (Figure 2-2a) and pull the magazine from the magazine well in the grip Figure 2-2b). Place the magazine in a pocket, magazine pouch or set it down.

**Figure 2-3a — Slide to the rear**          **Figure 2-3b — and press up on slide stop**

C. 1- Grip the serrations on the slide and (Figure 2-3a) 2- pull the slide rearward, allowing the round to extract and eject from the pistol. 3- Press up on the slide stop and release the tension on the slide to lock the slide to the rear (Figure 2-3b). Observe the round extracting and ejecting from the ejection port; do not attempt to retain the round.

**Figure 2-4a — Check the chamber**          **Figure 2-4b — Check the ejector**

D. Visually check the chamber for a round (Figure 2-4a) and check that the ejector is not broken (Figure 2-4b). Once you have ensured the pistol has no magazine in it and the chamber is free of ammunition, you now can close the slide by pulling the slide slightly to the rear and riding the slide forward so as not to forcefully shut on an empty chamber.

**Figure 2-5 — Unloaded and cleared pistol**

## Disassembling the Beretta Pistol

NOTE- Place the pistol's parts on a flat, clean surface with the muzzle oriented in a safe direction.

When the operator begins to disassemble the pistol, it should be done in the following order:

Field Strip-

    A.  Clear the pistol and leave the magazine out as described previously.

    B.  To remove the slide,

        1.  Pull back slide to release slide stop lever and close action to ensure it is in the battery position (Figure 2-6).

**Figure 2-6 — Slide forward and in battery**

        2.  Depress the takedown lever stop, which is the small button located of the right side of the frame in front of the trigger guard (Figure 2-7).

**Figure 2-7 — Takedown lever stop**

3. While holding the button down, rotate the takedown lever (located at the right side of the frame) downward about 90° (Figure 2-8).

**Figure 2-8 — Rotate the takedown lever down**

4. Pull the slide all the way forward and out of the frame (Figure 2-9a & 2-9b).

**Figure 2-9a — Slide forward**          **Figure 2-9b — Slide removed**

C. Remove the recoil spring assembly and barrel.

   1. Hold the slide by its milled grooves, sight pointed down (Figure 2-10).

**Figure 2-10 — Slide top down**

2. Push the recoil spring assembly slightly forward (towards muzzle) while lifting it away from the barrel (Figure 2-11). NOTE- While doing this you must maintain positive control to prevent guide rod from flying away due to the spring tension.

**Figure 2-11 — Remove recoil spring assembly**

3. Lift the barrel from the slide up and back out of the slide (Figure 2-12).

**Figure 2-12 — Remove barrel**

**Figure 2-13 — Field Stripped Beretta Pistol**

1- Slide
2- Barrel

3- Recoil Spring Assembly
4- Frame

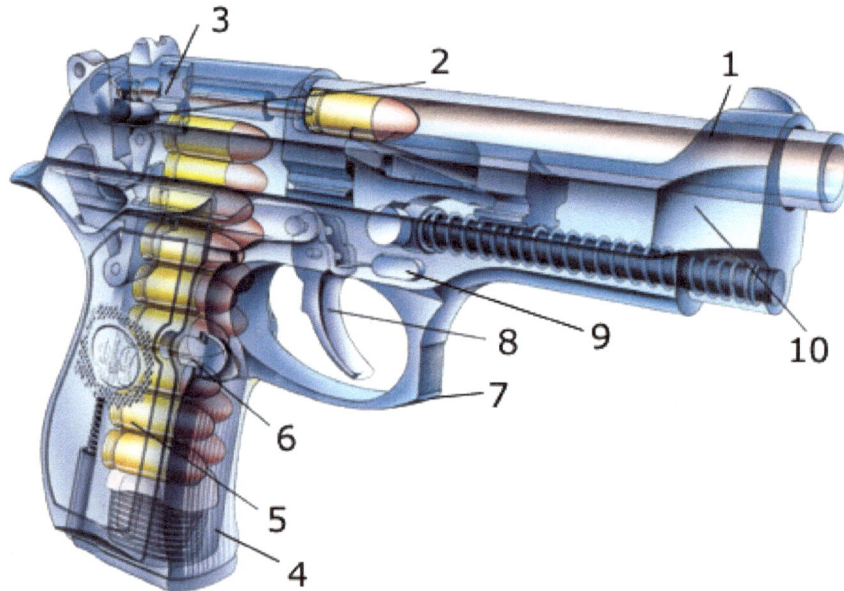

**Figure 2-14 — X-Ray of the Beretta Pistol**

1- Barrel
2- Safety
3- Firing Pin Block
4- Front Strap
5- Grip Panel

6- Magazine Release
7- Trigger Guard
8- Trigger
9- Takedown Lever Stop
10- Slide

## Disassemble the Beretta Magazine

A. Ensure the magazine is empty.

**Figure 2-15 — Removing the Magazine Floorplate**

B. With a punch or small screwdriver depress the locking plate under the magazine floorplate (Figure 2-15).

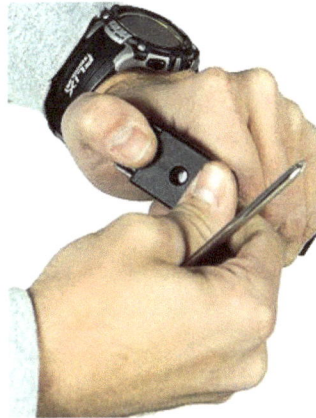

**Figure 2-16 — Slide off the magazine floorplate**
**NOTE-ensure to maintain pressure on the locking plate**

C. Carefully slide the floorplate off the magazine base while maintaining positive pressure onto the locking plate which is under spring pressure (Figure 2-16).

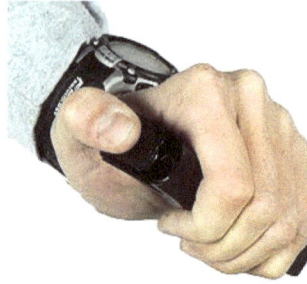

**Figure 2-17 — Maintain pressure on the locking plate**

D. Begin to let up on the locking plate and control the expansion of the magazine spring, point away from you as you do this (Figure2 2-17 and 2-18).

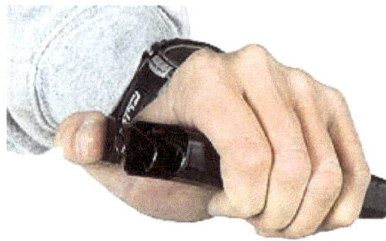

**Figure 2-18 — Remove the magazine spring from the magazine body**

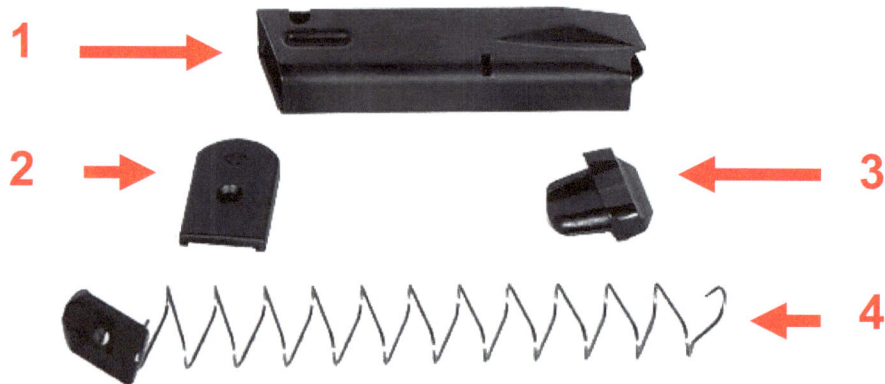

**Figure 2-19 — Disassemble Magazine**

1- Magazine Body      3- Follower
2- Floorplate      4- Spring and Locking Plate

E. Once disassembled clean prior to reassembling (Figure 2-19).

## Inspecting the Beretta Pistol

Once the pistol is disassembled and cleaned it should be thoroughly inspected for damage.

This inspection is for a **field stripped pistol**:

A. Barrel
   a. Barrel bulged
   b. Cracks at muzzle, locking block and or chamber
   c. Longitudinal cracks
   d. Condition of locking block

B. Slide
   a. Sights inspection
   b. Condition of the grooves
   c. Guide ring
   d. Cracks, especially under the ejection port
   e. Slide stop lever notch
   f. Brass deposits- clean
   g. Extractor clearance – clean

C. Frame
   a. Magazine catch
   b. Frame cracks
   c. Slide stop lever tension
   d. Condition of rails
   e. Slide lock (up and to the rear)

D. Recoil Spring Assembly
   a. Inspect for cracked guide rod

Once the pistol is reassembled perform an inspection of the following:

A. External visual inspection- overall condition

B. Safety check with safety on, no hammer movement

C. Trigger pull with safety on FIRE (should see and hear the hammer move rearward and release, maintain rearward pressure on the trigger and do step D)

D. Pull slide to the rear and release

E. Trigger reset check (release the trigger slowly to hear the reset "click") and refire trigger

F. Does an empty magazine lock the slide back?

**Points-**
- Do not disassemble the pistol past your ability to reassemble it so it will function properly.
- Watch for cracks and damage to the locking block as this has been found to be the weak part of the system.

## Reassembling the field stripped Beretta Pistol

A.  If you did not inspect the pistol parts during the cleaning it should be done during the reassembly.

B.  To reassemble the Beretta Pistol.

**Figure 2-20 — Insert barrel into slide**

1.  Insert the barrel (muzzle first) into the slide - down and in to the frame (Figure 2-20). Slide the barrel fully to the rear once fully down in the slide.

**Figure 2-21 — Insert the recoil spring assembly into the slide**

2.  Insert the recoil spring with guide rod into the dustcover and seat the guide rod into the barrel (the circular front section of the barrel) (Figure 2-21).

**Figure 2-22 — Lock the recoil spring assembly into the locking block**

20

3. Push the recoil spring assembly towards the muzzle slightly and place the rear of the assembly into the rounded cutout on the barrel (Figure 2-22). The assembly will be retained through its spring tension if properly placed. Do not leave on the flat non rounded cut out.

**Figure 2-23a — Start the slide on the rails and pull to the rear**

**Figure 2-23b — Rotate the takedown lever up into its locked position**

4. Turn the slide over so the sights are up and align the front rails on the receiver with the slide cutouts the rear of the slide. Once the slide is aligned pull the slide along the top of the receiver and to the full rearward position. Rotate the takedown lever back up and ease the slide forward and check for proper lock up. Slide should return to in battery position. (Figure 2-23a and 2-23b)

## Performing a Function Check on the Beretta Pistol

    A. External visual inspection- overall condition and ensure it is cleared of ammunition

    B. Trigger safety check with safety on, no hammer movement

    C. Trigger pull with safety on FIRE (should see and hear the hammer move rearward and release, maintain rearward pressure on the trigger and do step D)

    D. Pull slide to the rear and release

    E. Trigger reset check (release the trigger slowly to hear the reset "click") and refire trigger

    F. Does an empty magazine lock the slide back?

### Safeties on a Beretta Pistol

### 1. Firing Pin Safety

When the trigger is not pulled completely to the rear, a blocking device secures the firing pin and prevents it from moving forward. This safety for if the pistol is dropped and strikes the ground with the muzzle down (Figure 2-29).

**Figure 2-29 — Photo of the bar being lifted with trigger**

### 2. Manual Safety/Decocking Lever

This safety lever allows the hammer to be safely lowered over a loaded round in the chamber. The safety rotates to interrupt and shield the firing pin unit from a hammer strike. When the safety lever is on SAFE, the linkage between the trigger and sear are disconnected. (Figure 2-30a and 2-30b).

**Figure 2-30a — Safety being rotated**          **Figure 2-30b — Safety on SAFE**

## 3. Loaded Chamber Indicator

The extractor head protrudes when a cartridge is chambered and they extractor exposes a red warning signal. In the dark this protrusion may be felt to check the chamber condition. (Figure 2-31).

**Figure 2-31 — Photo of extractor sticking out with loaded chamber**

# Troubleshooting

When diagnosing malfunctions with the pistol, always start with the simplest and most likely cause.  Remember the acronym **SAMM-**

    **S**hooter (improper technique)
    **A**mmunition (incorrect or out of specification)
    **M**aintenance (dirty, unlubricated, or over lubricated)
    **M**echanical (broken or worn part)

These are the causes of malfunctions in the order they are most likely to occur.

| PROBLEM | PROBABLY CAUSES | CORRECTION |
|---|---|---|
| **Failure to extract** | Extractor worn/broken/missing | Replace |
| | Overpowered or underpowered Defective ammunition | Change ammunition |
| | Dirt under extractor claw | Clean extractor and check |
| | Dirty chamber | Clean chamber |
| | Shooting with an unlocked wrist | Lock wrists properly |
| **Failure to eject** | Broken or damaged ejector | Replace trigger mechanism with ejector |
| | Underpowered ammunition | Change ammunition |
| | Dirty chamber | Clean chamber |
| | Shooting with an unlocked wrist | Lock wrists properly |
| | Lack of lubrication | Lubricate as directed |
| | Dirty pistol | Clean and lubricate |
| **Failure to feed** | Magazine not properly inserted | Reinsert magazine |
| | Underpowered ammunition | Change ammunition |
| | Dirty chamber | Clean chamber |
| | Weak magazine spring | Replace |
| | Dirty chamber | Clean chamber |
| | Tight extractor | Replace or clean |
| | Shooting with an unlocked wrist | Lock wrists properly |
| | Deformed magazine | Replace magazine |
| | Weak recoil spring | Replace |
| **Slide fails to lock open on last round** | Magazine follower broken | Replace follower |
| | Dirty magazine | Clean |
| | Weak magazine spring | Replace |
| | Worn slide stop lever notch | Replace |
| | Dirty pistol | Clean |
| | Lack of lubrication | Lubricate as directed |
| | Deformed magazine | Replace magazine |
| | Improper grip | Thumb may be depressing the slide stop during firing, reposition thumb. |

24

| | Underpowered ammunition | Change ammunition |
| | Shooting with an unlocked wrist | Lock wrists properly |
| **Failure to fire** | Slide out of battery due to: | |
| | Deformed or defective round | Inspect and replace round |
| | Underpowered ammunition | Change ammunition |
| | Damaged or weak recoil spring | Replace |
| | Damaged recoil spring guide | Replace assembly |
| | Mating surfaces of barrel, slide and receiver excessively dirty | Field strip and clean |
| | Dirty gun or obstructed chamber | Clean |
| | Shooting with an unlocked wrist | Lock wrists properly |
| **No primer strike** | Worn or broken firing pin tip | Replace |
| | Obstructed firing pin channel | Clear |
| **Light, centered strike** | Hard primers (SMG ammo) | Change ammunition |
| | Obstructed firing pin channel | Remove, inspect, and clean firing pin. Clean firing pin channel |
| **Light off-centered strike** | Tight extractor | Replace |
| | Dirty pistol | Clean |
| | Slide lock reversed or not beveled | Replace |
| **Inconsistent trigger** | Pistol excessively dirty | Field strip and clean |
| | Needs lubrication | Lubricate |
| **Firing pin safety fails** | Damaged | Replace damaged part |
| **Locks open early** | Improper hand/thumb position | Grip properly |
| | Reverse tension on slide stop lever spring | Replace |
| | Damaged slide stop lever | Replace |

# Section 3

## Operation and Function

### Loading the Beretta Magazine

A. Ensure you have 9 x 19mm NATO ammunition; this ammunition is easily confused with 9 x 18mm (Makarov) and 9 x 17mm/.380 Automatic. Inspect it for uniformity, cleanliness, and serviceability. Check all cartridges for undented primers and only use issued ammunition.

**Figure 3-1b**      **Figure 3-1b**      **Figure 3-1c**
**Loading the magazine**

B. Use your non-dominant hand to hold the magazine with the rounded front of the magazine towards your fingertips. Your non-dominant thumb is used as a guide so as not to let the cartridge roll off the follower or other cartridges (Figure 3-1a). With your dominant hand, one at a time, begin with the base of the cartridge at the front of the magazine follower and press the cartridge down and back to insert (Figures 3-1b and 3-1c).

C. The Beretta magazines can hold various different round counts but due to overloading of the spring, do not carry the pistol loaded to capacity for long periods of time. Load the appropriate number of rounds and then load the chamber relieving the spring tension by one round. Placing a loose cartridge in the chamber and releasing the slide stop can cause damage to the extractor, so load the chamber from the magazine only.

### Loading the Beretta Pistol

26

**Figure 3-2 — Safe Direction**

A.  Start with a cleared pistol pointed in a safe direction. Place the pistol on SAFE (Figure 3-2).

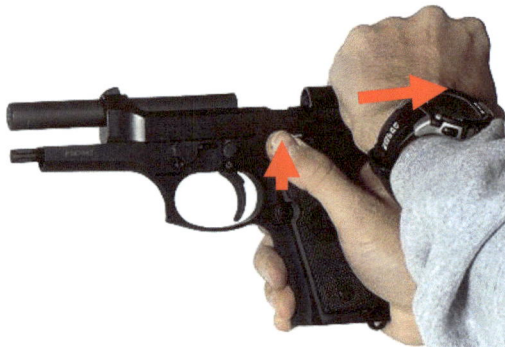

**Figure 3-3 — Locking the slide to the rear**

B.  Lock the slide by pulling it to the rear and pressing up on the slide stop (Figure 3-3). Once it is engaged, release the slide tension.

**Figure 3-4a**

**Figure 3-4b**

**Figure 3-4c**
**Inserting and seating the magazine**

C.  Insert the loaded magazine into the magazine well (Figures 3-4a and 3-4b). Fully seat the magazine with the heel of the hand to ensure it is locked in by the magazine catch (Figures 3-4c).

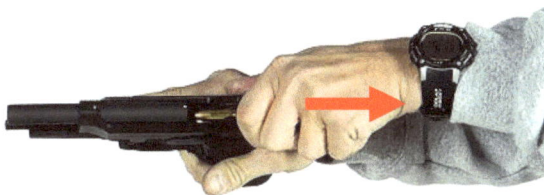

**Figure 3-5 — Cycle the slide**

D.  Pull the slide by gripping the serrations on the rear fully to rear, (not over the ejection port) and release allowing it to slam shut by its own spring tension (Figure 3-5). To ensure that a round has been chambered either removing the magazine to observe that one less rounds is in the counting windows on the back of the magazine, look at the loaded chamber indicator on the top of the extractor or perform a press check to observe the chambered casing through the ejection port. An alternative method of closing the slide to load is to press down on the slide stop and allow it to shut by its own spring tension. Ensure the slide is in battery (fully forward). Do not close the slide by pressing down on the slide stop unless there are cartridges in the magazine.

**Figure 3-6 — Ensure the pistol is decocked and on SAFE**

E. As the Beretta 92F is a single/double action pistol you can decock the pistol by placing the safety to SAFE (Figure 3-6). The internal safeties are all engaged.

## Firing the Beretta Pistol

**Figure 3-7 — Proper firing position**

A. Orient downrange in the direction of your targets or towards the threat.

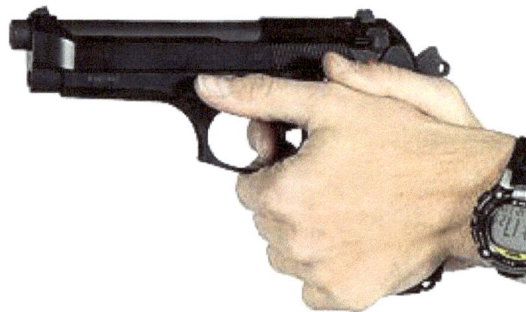

**Figure 3-8 — Taking up the slack of the trigger**

B. As you orient your sights onto the target, press the trigger straight back so as not to interrupt the sight picture (Figure 3-8). As the Beretta 92F is a double action/single action, you will notice your first shot will have a heavier trigger pressure than subsequent shots that are single action (hammer already to the rear). Remember to perform proper follow through and recovery and you should practice proper trigger reset to ensure light trigger pressure needed for subsequent shots.

**Figure 3-9 — When not shooting keep your trigger finger off the trigger**

C. When you have completed firing the pistol, remove your finger from the trigger and outside the trigger guard and decock the pistol. To decock press the safety from FIRE to SAFE and the firing pin will rotate out of the way and the hammer will safely drop (Figure 3-9).

# Section 4

## Performance Problems

### Malfunction and Immediate Action Procedures

Malfunctions are usually preventable through good practices, but they may still occur out of the blue from time to time. Of course, you hope it is on the practice range, but you should treat each one as you are in a life-or-death situation. Practicing proper and effective corrective actions will allow you to be more confident in your pistol handling. In stressful situations, you can become much more stressed due to an unforeseen malfunction that is easy to correct. I have observed many shooters that perceive themselves to be experienced, but when they encounter a stovepipe, they nearly disassemble the pistol rather than sweep it out and continue.

Malfunction drills must fix the problem 100% of the time (excluding a weapon stoppage—broken weapon) the first time performed. You must look at the pistol and identify the problem (obviously the pistol is not functioning as you need so you must transition to another weapon or rectify the situation) it is a non-function weapon at this point—fix it.

You should always practice taking a covered position to correct malfunctions with considerations on how you operate.

The following pages in this chapter describe and detail corrective actions for the various malfunctions that may be encountered.

**NOTE**: The <u>failure-to-go-into-battery malfunction</u>, when your slide does not fully return forward when cycling a round, is always rectified in the same manner, no matter which hand is being used. This malfunction is usually induced when loading and not allowing the full recoil spring tension to shut the slide.

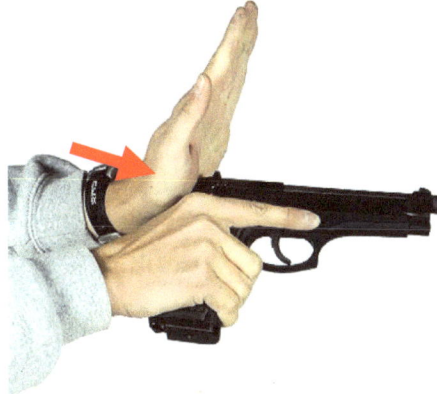

**Figure 4-1 — Seating the slide**

To fix a failure-to-go-into-battery malfunction, you must ensure your finger is off the trigger and outside the triggerguard and then slap the back of the slide with the heel of the non-firing hand (Figure 4-1). If you are shooting while wounded, then you will use your chest or equipment to force the slide forward into battery.

**FAILURE TO FIRE:** This malfunction occurs when the operator has loaded a dud cartridge or failed to load the chamber. The universal fix all for this is the "<u>Slap</u>, <u>Rack</u>, <u>Bang</u>" technique.

**SYMPTOM** - You perform a full presentation to shoot and hear and feel the hammer strike, and the weapon does not fire.

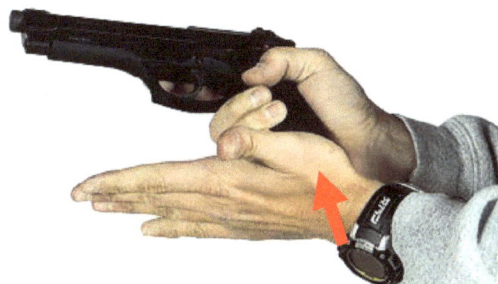

**Figure 4-2 — Slap**

1. **SLAP** the bottom of the magazine with a hard palm (fingers extended) to ensure it is fully seated and locked in (Figure 4-2).

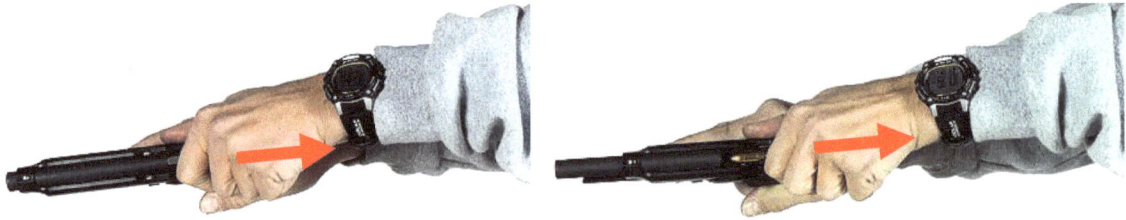

**Figure 4-3a**                 **Figure 4-3b**

**Rack**

2. **RACK** the slide fully to the rear and release it to shut by its own recoil spring tension (Figures 4-3a and 4-3b). You can pivot the slide toward your non-firing hand to assist in racking the slide to the rear; maintain muzzle to threat orientation.

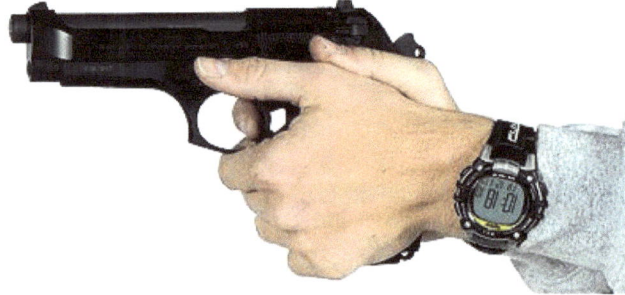

**Figure 4-4 — Ready/Bang**

3. **READY/BANG** or represent and prepare to fire the shot as you intended before the malfunction if your situation dictates that action (Figure 4-4).

**FAILURE TO EJECT:** This malfunction (commonly called a "stovepipe") is created usually by the slide being retarded (by not setting one's wrists- "limp wristing") in its rearward movement to rechamber the next round or a broken ejector. This malfunction can also be induced by an excessively dirty extractor which does not fully grip the rim of the cartridge during ejection. This malfunction is easily corrected by sweeping the expended case from the port. The corrective action is the same for vertical and horizontal stovepipes.

**Figure 4-5 — Stovepipe**

**SYMPTOM -** You are in the act of shooting a multiple-round engagement, and you notice you cannot see your front sight for a piece of brass is in the way, felt the slide did not fully close, and/or have a soft mushy trigger.

**Figure 4-6 — Reach across**          **Figure 4-7 — Rearward sweep**

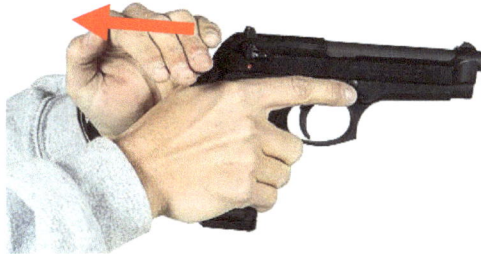

With the non-firing hand, extend your fingers, and with fingers joined, reach over the slide. (DO NOT SWEEP YOUR HAND IN FRONT OF THE MUZZLE.) Roll your fingers over the top of the slide with a firm, vigorous sweeping motion to the rear against the stuck casing to sweep it free (Figures 4-6 and 4-7). Do not sweep too far as you have to take more time to regrip and present.

Once the casing is no longer pinched by the slide, the slide will continue to seat the next round, and you are now ready to continue the engagement. Many inexperienced shooters do too much to correct this simple malfunction. **Ensure you do not work the slide fully to the rear when sweeping the empty casing**

**- this action could induce a double feed as the chamber is already loaded**. Continue the engagement as your situation dictates.

**NOTE**: You must always roll your fingers across so that whichever malfunction you encounter, vertical or horizontal, you will clear it with one sweep.

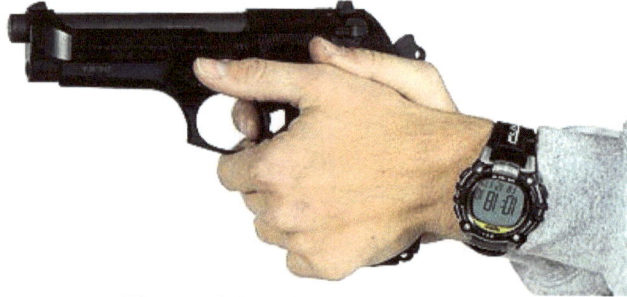

**Figure 4-8 — Present and fire**

**FAILURE TO EXTRACT:** This malfunction (commonly called a "double feed") is created when the spent casing is not extracted from the chamber, and the next round to be loaded is rammed from the magazine into the rear of the stuck casing (Figures 4-9 and 4-10). This malfunction is a serious one since more complicated dexterity is needed to correct it and, of course, to do it quickly. Below is the breakdown of the corrective action to restore your pistol back to operation.

**Figure 4-9 — Failure to Extract**

**SYMPTOM -** You are shooting a multiple-shot engagement and notice your slide did not go forward, you have a soft mushy trigger, and it will not fire.

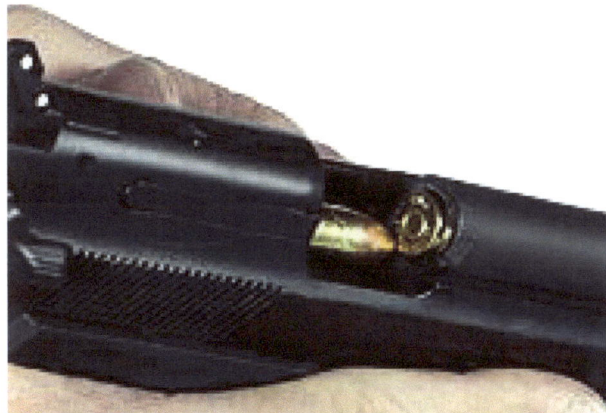

**Figure 4-10 — Failure to Extract malfunction**

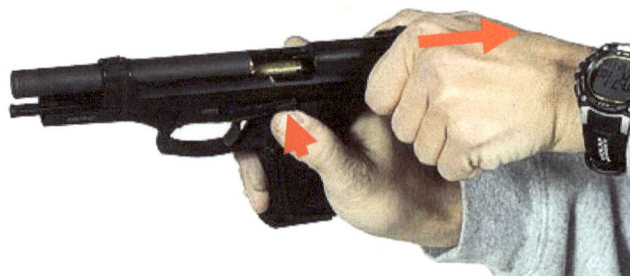

**Figure 4-11 — Step one of corrective actions**

**STEP ONE** - With your finger off the trigger, rotate the pistol in your firing hand so you may engage the slide stop with your firing hand thumb. With the non-firing hand, rack the slide to the rear and lock it with the slide stop by pushing it up into the notch, and let the recoil spring tension hold the slide stop in the notch (Figure 4-11).

**Figure 4-12 — Step two of corrective actions**

**STEP TWO** - Remove the magazine from the pistol (Figure 4-12).

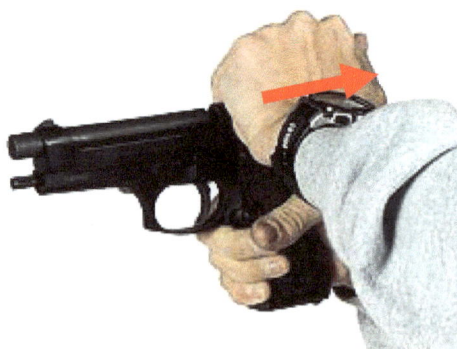

**Figure 4-13 — Step three of corrective actions**

**STEP THREE** - Rack the slide to the rear at least three times to ensure the casing is extracted and ejected from the pistol (Figure 4-13). As you are doing this step, observe the casing being ejected and allow the slide to use its force to shut each time it is pulled to the rear. You can rotate the slide towards your non-firing hand to assist in working the slide to the rear.

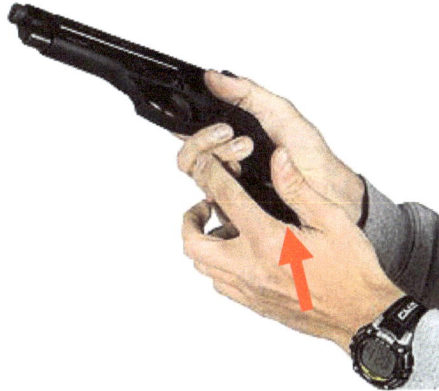

**Figure 4-14 — Step four of corrective actions**

**STEP FOUR** - Properly insert and seat a loaded magazine with a hard palm (Figure 4-14).

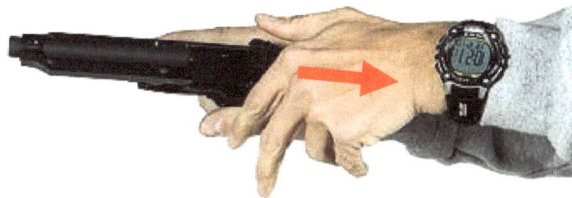

**Figure 4-15 — Step five of corrective actions**

**STEP FIVE** - Rack the slide fully to the rear and release it to close by its own spring tension (Figure 4-15). Your pistol is now ready to continue the engagement. You can rotate the slide towards your non-firing hand to assist in working the slide to the rear.

**Figure 4-16 — Step six of corrective actions**

**STEP SIX** - Continue the engagement as the situation dictates (Figure 4-16).

**NOTE**: Correcting this malfunction needs to be practiced often since it is the most complicated to do under stress or when you lose dexterity because blood is leaving the extremities.